Pedigree

Published 2008
Published by Pedigree Books LTD,
Beech Hill House, Walnut Gardens,
Exeter, Devon EX4 4DH
books@pedigreegroup.co.uk

£5.99

LUKE SKYWALKER

HOMEWORLD:	Tatooine
SPECIES:	Human
AFFILIATION:	Jedi
WEAPON:	Lightsaber, blaster pistol
VEHICLE:	X-wing starfighter, snowspeeder, T-16 skyhopper

EARLY YEARS

Luke Skywalker was born in the midst of some of the most dramatic events in the history of the galaxy. His destiny was tangled up with the fate of the Republic and the future of the tyrannical Empire. When his father turned to the dark side of the Force, his mother died from grief shortly after giving birth to Luke and his twin sister, Leia, who were immediately hidden away from his father and the Emperor.

Luke grew up as a simple farmboy on the backwater desert planet of Tatooine, working hard on his uncle's moisture farm. He was brought up by his aunt and uncle, Beru and Owen Lars. They told him that his father had been a navigator on a spice freighter, but the truth was that Anakin Skywalker had been a famous Jedi Knight and a gifted starpilot.

THE OUTSIDER

Luke learned about desert survival and droid repair on his uncle's farm, but his heart longed for adventure and excitement. He hung out around Tosche station in Anchorhead with a group of friends, but Luke never quite felt that he fitted in with them. The other boys sometimes teased him and called him 'Wormie'. His only true friend was Biggs Darklighter, and together they dreamed of one day joining the Imperial Academy.

Together, Luke and Biggs practiced their piloting skills in Tatooine's dangerous Beggar's Canyon. However, when the time came, Luke was not allowed to go to the Academy. His uncle needed him on the farm, and so when Biggs went away, Luke was stranded on Tatooine.

A GREAT JEDI

Luke's life changed forever when his uncle bought a pair of used droids from Jawa dealers. The droids, R2-D2 and C-3PO, took Luke on an adventure, leading him to Obi-Wan Kenobi and eventually to the discovery of his true identity. Luke's name would become known throughout the galaxy. Together with Princess Leia Organa and Han Solo, it was his destiny to destroy the evil Empire and restore peace to the galaxy.

YODA'S JEDI TRIALS

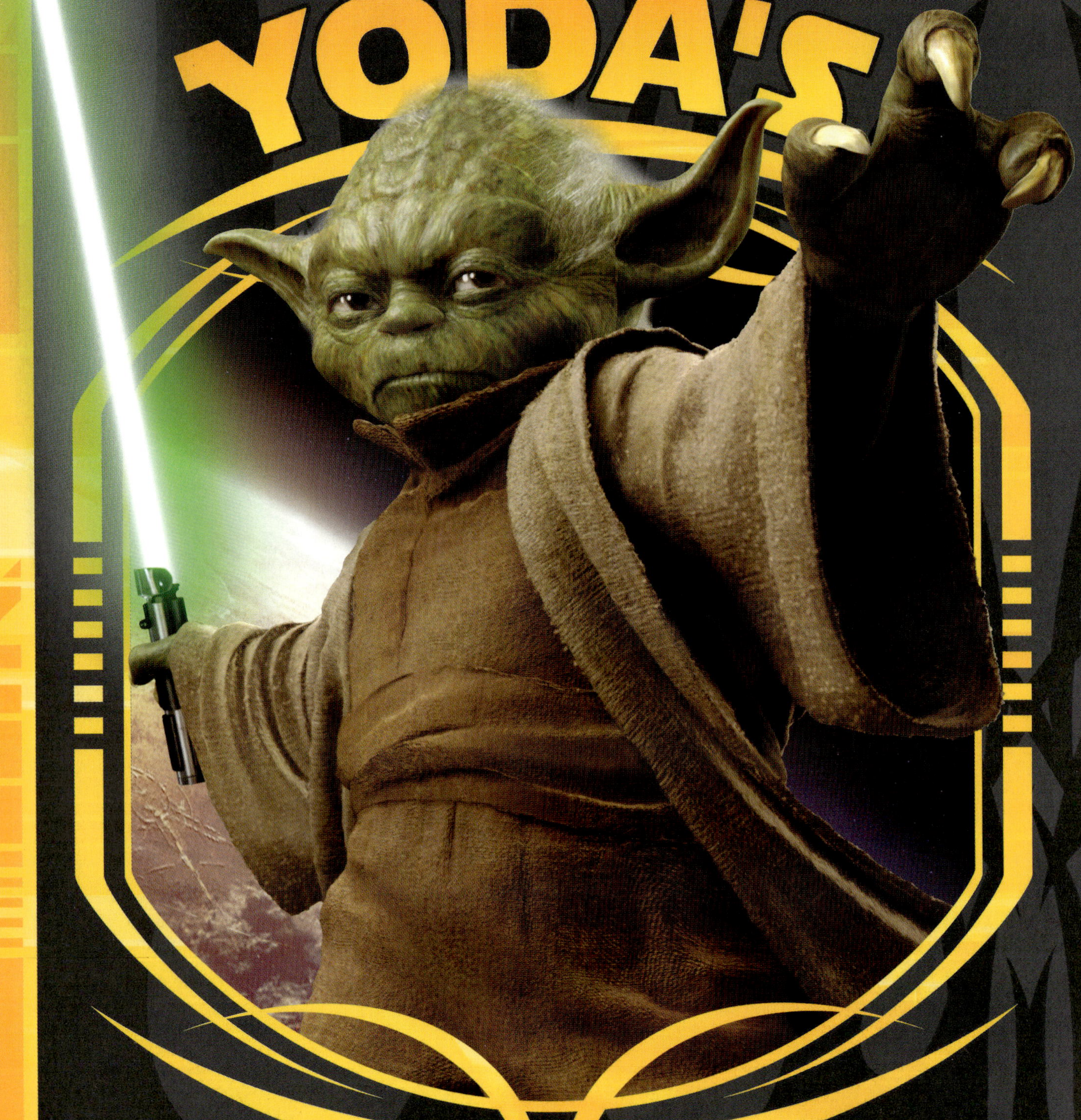

The path to becoming a Jedi Knight is a hard one. Many young Padawans will fail to reach their goal. Do you have what it takes to succeed? Clear your mind and feel the Force as you answer these questions.

Question 1

YOU ARE IN THE MIDDLE OF A VITAL TRAINING SESSION WHEN YOU SENSE THAT THERE IS SOMETHING WRONG WITH YOUR FAMILY AT HOME. WHAT DO YOU DO?

- A :: CONTINUE THE TRAINING SESSION ☐
- B :: RUSH HOME AT ONCE ☐
- C :: EXPLAIN TO YOUR MASTER WHY YOU CANNOT CONCENTRATE ☐

Question 2

WHAT DO YOU VALUE MOST HIGHLY?

- A :: YOUR CONNECTION WITH THE FORCE ☐
- B :: YOUR LIGHTSABER ☐
- C :: YOUR FAMILY ☐

Question 3

A SITH LORD IS TRYING TO TEMPT YOU TO THE DARK SIDE. HOW DO YOU RESIST?

- A :: YOU FOCUS ON HOW EVIL HE IS ☐
- B :: YOU FOCUS ON THE LIGHTSABER BATTLE ☐
- C :: YOU FOCUS ON LETTING THE FORCE FLOW THROUGH YOU ☐

Question 4

WHAT GETS YOU MOST EXCITED?

- A :: LEARNING NEW SKILLS IN THE FORCE ☐
- B :: BEING AT ONE WITH THE FORCE ☐
- C :: SEEING OLD FRIENDS ☐

Question 5

YOU DISCOVER THAT YOUR FRIEND IS PLOTTING TO DESTROY EVERYTHING YOU MOST VALUE. HOW DO YOU REACT?

- A :: YOU ARE ANGRY AND YOU RUSH TO CONFRONT HIM ☐
- B :: YOU CANNOT BELIEVE IT, AND YOU NEED TIME TO THINK IT THROUGH ☐
- C :: YOU INFORM YOUR MASTER AT ONCE ☐

Question 6

WHAT DO YOU LIKE MOST ABOUT YOURSELF?

- A :: THE JEDI SKILLS THAT ENABLE YOU TO HELP OTHERS ☐
- B :: YOUR LOVE FOR YOUR FRIENDS AND FAMILY ☐
- C :: YOUR STATUS AS A JEDI ☐

ADD UP YOUR SCORE...

... AND CARRY THEM ON TO THE NEXT CHALLENGE.

1	A = 10	B = 2	C = 6
2	A = 10	B = 6	C = 2
3	A = 2	B = 6	C = 10
4	A = 2	B = 10	C = 6
5	A = 2	B = 6	C = 10
6	A = 10	B = 6	C = 2

WRITE DOWN YOUR SCORE HERE!

....

PERSONAL PROFILE

STICK YOUR PHOTO HERE!

NAME >> ....

SPECIES >> ....

HOME PLANET >> ....

HEIGHT >> ....

WEIGHT >> ....

SPECIAL FEATURES >> ....

WEAPON >> ....

VEHICLE >> ....

AFFILIATION >> ....

FRIENDS >> ....

PADAWAN STATUS >> ....

AMBITIONS >> ....

SKILLS >> ....

GREATEST FEAR >> ....

HAPPIEST MOMENT >> ....

PETS/DROIDS >> ....

JEDI ROLE MODEL >> ....

THREE WORDS THAT BEST DESCRIBE YOU

>> ....

>> ....

>> ....

NUTE GUNRAY

HOMEWORLD:	Neimoidia
SPECIES:	Neimoidian
AFFILIATION:	Trade Federation
VEHICLE:	Trade Federation Battleship, Neimoidian shuttle

Ruthless Nute Gunray was the unscrupulous Viceroy of the Trade Federation who led the blockade and invasion of Naboo. He was secretly under the control of the Sith Lord, Darth Sidious, and he hoped that this would bring him power and wealth.

Gunray was a bully, but he was also a coward. When Naboo freedom fighters stormed the Royal Palace, Gunray cowered behind his troops, willing to sacrifice anyone and anything to save his own skin. Queen Amidala broke into her own palace and blasted through Gunray's protectors. The greedy Viceroy was arrested at gunpoint and taken away to answer for his crimes.

However, the Republic was riddled with corruption, and Gunray was able to buy his way to safety through the legal system. After four trials in the Supreme Court, Gunray still held his position of Viceroy.

Gunray later allied himself with Count Dooku. He promised to become part of the new Confederacy of Independent Systems and continued to believe the visions of riches and conquest that Darth Sidious promised him. However, at the end of the war he was no longer useful to the evil Emperor of the galaxy. Darth Sidious sent Darth Vader to kill Gunray and all the other Separatist barons. Gunray died at Vader's hand.

HOME SWEET HOME

CAN YOU MATCH EACH OF THESE FAMOUS CHARACTERS TO THEIR HOME PLANET?

BAIL ORGANA

CHEWBACCA

COUNT DOOKU

JABBA THE HUTT

- ALDERAAN
- ENDOR'S FOREST MOON
- KAMINO
- KASHYYYK
- NABOO
- NEIMOIDIA
- SERENNO
- TATOOINE

JAR JAR BINKS

LAMA SU

NUTE GUNRAY

WICKET W. WARRICK

DARK SIDE WORD SEARCH

SEEK OUT ALL TEN DARK SIDE-WORDS IN THIS WORDSEARCH. ANSWERS CAN BE FORWARDS, BACKWARDS, VERTICAL, HORIZONTAL OR DIAGONAL.

a	f	d	e	r	e	h	s	d	g	e	b	k	m	h
c	b	h	a	i	k	e	r	h	d	n	c	n	a	m
e	m	g	n	i	n	t	h	g	i	l	d	s	o	i
i	h	o	b	o	e	f	g	b	i	c	r	b	k	a
f	l	b	l	j	h	c	i	k	a	e	e	d	i	d
b	h	c	o	d	t	g	e	m	p	e	r	o	r	k
q	e	r	b	f	i	g	i	o	k	b	f	c	e	a
k	m	d	j	h	s	q	o	c	e	a	g	f	g	n
j	p	g	d	h	l	r	b	j	i	d	a	e	n	j
b	i	q	h	e	t	m	d	f	l	o	m	g	a	f
e	r	g	q	m	i	b	a	c	j	o	i	e	h	n
q	e	h	r	a	e	f	e	g	f	k	f	r	a	l
o	l	o	q	g	r	i	e	v	o	u	s	c	r	e
h	t	j	b	n	e	r	j	e	r	f	c	l	j	i
s	q	k	g	j	a	f	l	i	b	n	o	a	k	c

- anger
- clones
- dooku
- emperor
- empire
- fear
- grievous
- lightning
- sith
- stormtoopers

TECHNICAL DESIGN

USE THIS GRID TO MAKE YOUR OWN TECHNICAL DRAWING OF THE LEGENDARY

MILLENNIUM FALCON!

SHMI SKYWALKER

SPECIES:	HUMAN
HEIGHT:	1.63 METRES

Shmi Skywalker was a slave, but she wanted a better life for her son, Anakin. She was gentle and loving, and she knew that he was very special. When Anakin was a toddler, they became the property of Gardulla the Hutt and went to live in Mos Espa on Tatooine. Eventually, Watto, a Toydarian, became their owner. He worked them hard but also allowed them some privacy.

When Anakin was nine, a Naboo delegation was stranded on Tatooine. Generously, Anakin offered them shelter in the small hovel the Skywalkers called home. The delegation was led by Jedi Master Qui-Gon Jinn, who sensed that the Force was very strong in Anakin.
He could not free Shmi, but he could offer her son a better life. Shmi said a heartbreaking goodbye to Anakin, knowing that his future lay in the stars beyond Tatooine. Watto was addicted to gambling and eventually he was

forced to sell Shmi. A moisture farmer named Cliegg Lars had fallen in love with her, and bought her freedom. They married and Shmi became stepmother to Cliegg's son, Owen. They lived a quiet, happy life as moisture farmers. However, Shmi often looked up at the stars and thought of her son.

One early morning, Shmi left the safety of the house to gather mushrooms. She was attacked and kidnapped by a raiding party of Tusken Raiders. Cliegg rounded up a posse of moisture farmers to rescue her, but the Tuskens attacked them too. Only four of the 30 farmers returned, including a maimed Cliegg.

A month later, Anakin arrived at the Lars homestead. Cliegg told him what had happened, but Anakin refused to accept that his mother was dead. He raced into the desert in search of her.

Amakin found his mother as she was dying. She had been badly treated by the Tuskens, and she died in her son's arms. Anakin, filled with rage and grief, vanquished all the Tuskens and then took his mother's body and buried her at the Lars homestead. He felt ashamed that he had not been able to protect her, and vowed that he would never fail again.

MAKE A YODA MASK

FOLLOW THE INSTRUCTIONS TO MAKE A MASK OF ONE OF THE GREATEST JEDI MASTERS OF ALL TIME.

YOU WILL NEED:

- Scissors (and an adult to help you)
- Green paper
- Pencil Glue
- Crayons, paints or felt tips
- Long green pipe cleaners
- Cotton wool

WHAT TO DO:

1. Trace the template on to your green paper.
2. Cut the shape out. Be very careful when you cut out the eyes.
3. Put some glue on the top of the head and attach a few wisps of cotton wool to make Yoda's hair.
4. Use your paints, crayons or felt tips to give Yoda his mouth, lines and wrinkles.
5. Gently punch a pipe cleaner through the side of the mask and twist it closed. Repeat on the other side with another pipe cleaner.
6. Put your mask against your face and fasten the two pipe cleaners together at the back of your head!

PADMÉ AMIDALA

Obi-Wan Kenobi

DARTH MAUL

HOMEWORLD:	Iridonia
SPECIES:	Zabrak
WEAPON:	Sith lightsaber
VEHICLE:	Sith Infiltrator, Sith speeder
AFFILIATION:	Sith

Darth Maul was Darth Sidious's young and deadly apprentice. He was brought up to be a weapon, knowing only harsh, abusive training. Darth Maul became an incredible warrior and a creature of pure evil. His entire body was covered in detailed Sith tattoos, and his only goal was to wreak revenge on the Jedi for nearly destroying the Sith a millennium prior.

It was important to hide the Sith presence from the Jedi, so all Maul's missions were done in the shadows. Maul longed to reveal the Sith menace to the Jedi, but he was devoted to his Master and he obeyed orders.

Maul's Sith Infiltrator was a modified star courier vessel equipped with a cloaking device. His Sith speeder had no weapons – it was kept as simple as possible in order to deliver maximum speed.

Darth Maul attacked the Jedi Master Qui-Gon Jinn

on the planet Tatooine. Qui-Gon was utterly surprised and unprepared for such an attack. Like everyone else, he thought that the Sith had been completely wiped out a millennium before. However, this attacker had a double-ended lightsaber and was a highly skilled warrior.

Darth Maul was sent by Darth Sidious to track down Queen Amidala, and he eventually found himself in battle with *two* Jedi warriors on Naboo. He killed Qui-Gon with a fearsome lightsaber strike and then turned on Obi-Wan Kenobi. Their duel was lightning fast and fierce, and Obi-Wan briefly allowed himself to become enraged. However, in the end Obi-Wan was able to calm himself and call upon the light side of the Force to help him. He cut the evil Sith in half with his lightsaber. Darth Sidious would have to find a new apprentice.

THE CHOSEN ONE

How well do you know the history of the dramatic fall of the Republic and the Jedi Order? This is the story of how Anakin Skywalker met a Jedi Knight and joined the Order. Can you put the missing words in the correct places?

- TATOOINE
- SHMI
- OBI-WAN KENOBI
- WATTO
- FORCE
- SITH
- JEDI
- CORUSCANT
- PODRACE

Jedi Knight Qui-Gon Jinn and his apprentice, 1 ________ are sent to the planet Naboo to settle a dispute between the Trade Federation and Queen Amidala. Unknown to the Galactic Senate, the Federation has formed an alliance with Darth Sidious, a 2 ________ Lord.

The Viceroy tries to kill the two Jedi, but they escape and meet Jar Jar Binks, a Gungan. He helps them to find Queen Amidala. They rescue her and set off for 3 ________, the galactic seat of government, to get help.

They land on the desert planet 4 ________ to repair their damaged ship. At a junk shop, they meet Anakin Skywalker, a young slave boy. 5 ________, Anakin's owner, wants a lot of money for the part Qui-Gon needs to repair his ship.

Qui-Gon senses that the 6 ________ is incredibly strong with Anakin. He believes that the boy may be the Chosen One, who is destined to return balance to the Force.

To help Qui-Gon get the money he needs, Anakin enters his own Podracer in a dangerous 7 ________. Qui-Gon makes a bet with Watto. If Anakin wins, he will be free. If he loses, Watto will get the Queen's ship.

Anakin wins and Watto frees him. Wanting a better life for her son, his mother 8 ________ allows Anakin to leave with Qui-Gon to become a 9 ________.

The Jedi have been tracked to Tatooine by Darth Maul, who is 10 ____________'s apprentice. He attacks them, but they escape and continue their journey.

When Qui-Gon tells the Jedi 11 ____________ about the Sith, they can hardly believe it. They refuse to allow Qui-Gon to train Anakin as a Jedi. They say that he is too old. Master 12 ____________ has also sensed something dangerous in him. Qui-Gon defies them and says that he will make Anakin his 13 ____________.

Queen Amidala feels angry that the Senate is not moving quickly to help Naboo. Senator 14 ____________ tells her that Supreme Chancellor 15 ____________ is a weak leader. He persuades her to call for a vote of no confidence against the Supreme Chancellor, and he is removed from office. Palpatine is nominated to replace him. Queen Amidala returns to Naboo with Qui-Gon, Obi-Wan, Jar Jar and Anakin.

With Jar Jar's help, Amidala makes an alliance with the 16 ____________. They prepare to fight the Federation droid army. While the Queen and the Jedi break into the palace, Anakin hides in the cockpit of a starfighter.

Darth Maul is waiting for the two Jedi. Qui-Gon and Obi-Wan prepare to fight him while the Queen goes to find the Viceroy. He is in the 17 ____________, and she and her troops overpower him.

Darth Maul kills Qui-Gon, but Obi-Wan uses the Force to defeat the evil Sith. Meanwhile, the Gungans are losing against the massive droid army.

Anakin accidentally takes off in the starfighter and lands inside the droid control ship, which is in the sky above Naboo. Anakin fires a 18 ____________ at a reactor and destroys the ship. The computer-controlled droid army is deactivated, the battle is over and the 19 ____________ has lost.

Senator Palpatine is elected Supreme Chancellor of the 20 ____________. Obi-Wan is promoted to 21 ____________ and the Council agrees to make Anakin his Padawan. The Council reluctantly agrees.

- PADAWAN
- GALACTIC REPUBLIC
- VALORUM
- GUNGANS
- TORPEDO
- YODA
- COUNCIL
- PALPATINE
- TRADE FEDERATION
- JEDI KNIGHT
- DARTH SIDIOUS
- THRONE ROOM

SPOT THE DIFFERENCE

A JEDI NEEDS EAGLE-EYED VISION. THERE ARE EIGHT DIFFERENCES BETWEEN THESE TWO PHOTOGRAPHS. CAN YOU FIND THEM ALL?

STAR MAZE

Luke and R2-D2 must find their way through the galaxy to the Dagobah system, where Yoda is waiting. Can you help them navigate through the stars, keeping away from Imperial fighters?

QUI-GON JINN

SPECIES:	Human
HEIGHT:	1.93 metres
WEAPON:	Lightsaber
AFFILIATION:	Jedi

Qui-Gon Jinn believed in living for the moment and trusting his instincts. His failure with his second Padawan student, Xanatos, made him refuse to take on any more Padawans. Xanatos was the son of Crion, the wealthiest man on the planet Telos. Though he had great potential as a Jedi, his high birth and attitude often led to clashes with his fellow students. For Xanatos' final test, he had to return to Telos with Qui-Gon. A civil war was brewing, and Xanatos' father begged him for help controlling the planet. Xanatos agreed, and Qui-Gon found himself at war with his own student.

Qui-Gon killed Crion in battle, and then defeated Xanatos. However, he could not bear to kill his own Padawan and the student fled. Qui-Gon vowed never again to train a Padawan. However, after many years, Yoda managed to persuade Qui-Gon to take on a Padawan.

Obi-Wan Kenobi became his third apprentice. Together they became a formidable team.

It was thanks to Qui-Gon that Anakin Skywalker became a Jedi Knight. He discovered Anakin as a young slave boy on Tatooine, and realized that he was strong in the Force. He liberated Anakin from slavery and took him to Coruscant to present him to the Jedi Council. The Council refused to allow Qui-Gon to train Anakin, but the Jedi Master nevertheless kept the boy as his ward as he returned to Naboo.

Qui-Gon's last battle was with the Sith Darth Maul on Naboo. Maul was a fearsome opponent. Qui-Gon became separated from Obi-Wan during the course of the battle. Maul used this to his advantage and delivered a deadly blow to the Jedi Master. Obi-Wan defeated Maul, but nothing could save Qui-Gon. With his last breath, the Jedi Master asked Obi-Wan to train Anakin Skywalker.

Qui-Gon's body was cremated at a funeral attended by numerous mourners, including Anakin, Obi-Wan, Jar Jar Binks and several Jedi Council members.

SITH CROSSWORD

FOCUS YOUR MIND POWERS AND SOLVE THESE MYSTERIOUS CLUES.

ACROSS

2. A Jedi Knight who turned to the dark side.
4. It is the path to the dark side.
7. The planet where the clone army was created.
8. The Empire's ultimate weapon of destruction.

DOWN

1. This bounty hunter brought Han Solo to Jabba the Hutt.
3. The Emperor's Sith name.
5. The Sith Lord who killed Obi-Wan Kenobi.
6. The Force ______ is a dark side weapon.

SUDOKU

Test your mind powers with this fiendishly difficult Sudoku puzzle.

The lines of squares running horizontally are called rows, and the lines running vertically are called columns. The grid is further divided by the darker lines into nine 3 X 3 square 'boxes'. Some of the squares already have numbers in them. The task is to fill in the blank squares. Each row, column and box must end up containing all of the numbers from 1 to 9, and each number can only appear once in a row, column or box.

5							3	
6			4			8		
		7	3					9
	2	8			1			4
	5							1
			7	9				
9					6	3		
				8		5		
		2			3	7		

YODA'S

JEDI TRIALS

You have reached the second stage of your training. You have achieved much, but harder tasks lie ahead.

Question 7

You have tracked a mysterious assassin to an unknown planet. How do you proceed?

- A :: CONTACT THE JEDI COUNCIL TO GET THEIR ORDERS ☐
- B :: CONFRONT THE ASSASSIN ☐
- C :: FOLLOW THE ASSASSIN AND TRY TO WIN HIS CONFIDENCE ☐

Question 8

You have a nightmare that you suspect prophesies the future. Do you tell your Master about it?

- A :: NOT YET – YOU WANT TO RESEARCH THE POWER OF DREAMS TO LEARN IF YOU SHOULD BE CONCERNED ☐
- B :: NO – IT IS NONE OF HIS BUSINESS ☐
- C :: YES – YOU WANT HIS ADVICE ☐

Question 9

You are the best pilot among the Padawans and some of them ask you to put on a display of your skills. Do you accept?

- A :: NO ☐
- B :: YES ☐
- C :: YOU CAN'T DECIDE ☐

Question 10

Do you believe that your appearance matters?

- A :: NO – IT IS WHAT IS INSIDE THAT IS IMPORTANT ☐
- B :: YES – IF YOU DRESS SMARTLY, IT SHOWS THAT YOUR THOUGHTS ARE ORDERLY AND FOCUSED ☐
- C :: YES – YOU NEED TO CREATE THE RIGHT IMPRESSION ON OTHERS ☐

Question 11

How often do you use your Jedi mind tricks to control others?

- A :: PROBABLY A BIT TOO OFTEN ☐
- B :: NEVER – I PREFER NOT TO USE MY POWERS ON OTHERS ☐
- C :: RARELY – ONLY WHEN THE SITUATION MAKES IT NECESSARY ☐

Question 12

Your Master has begun to rely on you and trust you. How does that make you feel?

- A :: PROUD TO BE SO IMPORTANT TO HIM ☐
- B :: CONCERNED – YOU HOPE THAT YOU DON'T LET HIM DOWN ☐
- C :: SATISFIED THAT YOUR TRAINING IS PROGRESSING AS IT SHOULD ☐

ADD UP YOUR SCORE...

... FROM THIS ROUND AND THEN MOVE ON TO THE LAST STAGE OF YOUR TRAINING.

7.	A=10	B=2	C=6
8.	A=6	B=2	C=10
9.	A=10	B=2	C=6
10.	A=10	B=6	C=2
11.	A=2	B=6	C=10
12.	A=2	B=6	C=10

WRITE DOWN YOUR SCORE HERE!

....

JANGO FETT

HOMEWORLD:	Concord Dawn
SPECIES:	Human
WEAPONS:	Mandalorian battle armour, twin blaster pistols
VEHICLE:	*Slave I*
AFFILIATION:	None (bounty hunter)

In the final years of the Republic, Jango Fett was the best bounty hunter in the galaxy. He was a skilled marksman and unarmed fighter. Fett wore a sleek armoured suit that hid his scarred face and strangely tattooed arms. His combat gear included retractable wrist blades, a snare and dual blaster pistols.

Jango used a harnessed jetpack to gain the advantage of speed and height over his enemies. The backpack also carried an explosive rocket.

About a decade before the Clone Wars began, a man called Tyranus approached Jango with an unusual proposal. He offered Jango a huge amount of money to become the template of a clone army. Fett agreed, on the condition that he could have an unaltered clone of himself. Unlike the other clones, this one would not undergo growth acceleration or docility tampering. It would be a pure

replica of Jango. Jango lived on Kamino, teaching his son, the unaltered clone he named Boba, the ropes of survival and combat while the Kaminoans extracted genetic material to build thousands of clone soldiers. When Obi-Wan Kenobi arrived on Kamino, Jango decided it was time to leave. He and Boba escaped aboard *Slave I* and fled to Geonosis.

During the first battle of the Clone Wars, Jango fought against the Jedi. His blaster skills killed several Jedi, but he was no match for Mace Windu. The Jedi Master deflected Jango's blasts and cut off the bounty hunter's head with a single stroke of his lightsaber. Boba Fett was left an orphan.

SPACE RACE

ANSWER THESE QUESTIONS TO DISCOVER WHICH SPECIES YOU WOULD BE.

HOW TALL ARE YOU?

A :: SKYSCRAPER ☐
B :: AVERAGE ☐
C :: YOU CAN'T SEE OVER THE DINING TABLE ☐

WHERE WOULD YOU PREFER TO LIVE?

A :: OUTER SPACE ☐
B :: THE CITY ☐
C :: THE COUNTRY ☐

WHICH WORD DESCRIBES YOU BEST?

A :: BRAVE ☐
B :: CUNNING ☐
C :: KIND ☐

Where would you be during a battle?

A :: IN THE FRONT LINE
B :: HIDING UNTIL IT WAS OVER
C :: PROVIDING BACK UP

How do you feel about computers?

A :: THEY USUALLY WORK IF I HIT THEM HARD ENOUGH
B :: I CAN DO ANYTHING ON A COMPUTER
C :: I TRY TO STAY AWAY FROM THEM

How would you describe your temper?

A :: RED HOT BUT OVER IN A FLASH
B :: I NEVER SHOUT BUT I HOLD A GRUDGE FOREVER
C :: I DON'T HAVE A BAD TEMPER

Which destination most attracts you?

A :: DESERT
B :: SEA
C :: RAINFOREST

Which is closest to your ambition?

A :: SOLDIER
B :: BUSINESS EXECUTIVE
C :: FARMER

Answers

MOSTLY As:
You are a Wookiee. Intelligent, sophisticated, loyal and brave, you will fight fiercely to defend your friends, but in peaceful times you are tender and gentle.

MOSTLY Bs:
You are a Neimoidian. Although you are bold and aggressive in business, you tend to put yourself first.

MOSTLY Cs:
You are an Ewok. You are curious and a quick learner. You are a spiritual person and you enjoy a good celebration, but you will defend those you love bravely.

C-3PO'S RIDDLER

EXERCISE YOUR MIND WITH THESE BRAIN-TEASING RIDDLES.

1 What was given to you and belongs to you, but is used more by your friends than by you?

2 What is as big as a bantha but weighs nothing?

3 What has a big mouth but doesn't say a word?

4 What goes up and down stairs without moving?

5 What goes around the world and stays in a corner?

6 I have holes on the top, bottom, left and right, but I can hold water. What am I?

7 What can fill up a room but take up no space?

8 Give it food and it will live; give it water and it will die. What is it?

9 What kind of room has no windows or doors?

10 Light as a feather, there is nothing in it; the strongest man can't hold it for much more than a minute.

11 I went into the woods and got it, I sat down to seek it, I brought it home with me because I couldn't find it.

12 What kind of coat can be put on only when wet?

13 What question can you never answer 'yes' to?

CHANGING WORDS

FIND THE PATH FROM ONE WORD TO ANOTHER BY CHANGING JUST ONE LETTER AT A TIME.
(THE WORDS YOU CREATE ALONG THE WAY MUST ALL BE REAL WORDS.)

EXAMPLE: BOAT TO HEAD

BOAT — Beat — Heat — **HEAD**

1: SITH .... HIDE

2: SHIP .... THIS

3: FEAR .... MEAN

4: STAR .... BEAM

5: LOVE .... BOND

6: CLONE .... PROVE

7: SPACE .... SMELL

JAR JAR BINKS

HOMEWORLD:	Naboo
SPECIES:	Gungan
WEAPON:	Gungan boomer
VEHICLE:	Kaadu
AFFILIATION:	Gungan Grand Army, Galactic Senate, Galactic Republic

Jar Jar Binks was exiled from the underwater city of Otoh Gunga and spent his time in the Naboo swampland, living on raw shellfish or anything else that the murky ecosystem had to offer. However, when a Jedi Knight Qui-Gon Jinn saved his life, Jar Jar owed him a debt. He guided Qui-Gon and Obi-Wan Kenobi to Otoh Gunga, and became instrumental in liberating Naboo.

Although his bungling mannerisms constantly landed him in trouble, his loyal nature and kindness helped him to triumph in the end. Jar Jar eventually became a Senior Representative for Naboo, serving alongside Padmé Amidala. He was compassionate and meant well, but his trusting nature was easily exploited by corrupt politicians.

Jar Jar was a member of the Loyalist Committee, a group of Senators who wanted to find a peaceful way of stopping the Separatist movement spreading throughout the galaxy. However, when Senator Amidala was forced to flee the capital, Jar Jar was tricked into proposing the motion to give emergency powers to Supreme Chancellor Palpatine. This decision would have devastating consequences for the Republic.

STORY TELLER

HOW WELL DO YOU KNOW ANAKIN SKYWALKER'S LIFE STORY? USE A MARKER PEN TO LINK THE EVENTS IN THE CORRECT ORDER.

1 :: Becomes Obi-Wan Kenobi's Padawan.

2 :: Becomes Palpatine's Sith apprentice.

3 :: Destroys the Tusken tribe that killed his mother.

4 :: Duels with Obi-Wan Kenobi on Mustafar.

5 :: ESCORTS PADMÉ AMIDALA TO NABOO.

6 :: HELPS TO SAVE NABOO BY DESTROYING THE DROID CONTROL SHIP ABOVE THE PLANET.

7 :: DESTROYS THE EMPEROR.

8 :: MARRIES PADMÉ AMIDALA.

9 :: MEETS QUI-GON JINN AND PADMÉ AMIDALA.

10 :: MURDERS THE YOUNGLINGS IN THE JEDI TEMPLE.

11 :: TELLS LUKE SKYWALKER HIS TRUE IDENTITY.

12 :: TORTURES PRINCESS LEIA ORGANA.

GENERAL GRIEVOUS

HOMEWORLD:	KALEE
SPECIES:	KALEESH
WEAPONS:	LIGHTSABERS, BLASTER PISTOL, ELECTROSTAFF
VEHICLE:	WHEEL BIKE, STARFIGHTER, TRADE FEDERATION CRUISER
AFFILIATION:	CONFEDERACY OF INDEPENDENT SYSTEMS

General Grievous was a brave and brilliant strategist without a shred of compassion. Long before the Clone Wars, he had a horrible accident and very nearly died. In order to live, he allowed the Geonosians to make a durasteel shell for what little of him remained.

Grievous hunted Jedi for sport and kept his victims' lightsabers as trophies of his conquests. His indestructible body gave him the edge in battle. Each of his six-fingered arms could split in two, giving him four limbs, each armed with a lightsaber. Grievous could spin these arms in a whirling storm of light.

Only against opponents he deemed worthy did he enter into combat. He was trained in lightsaber arts by Darth Tyranus (Count Dooku), and his ingenuity and cunning made him almost invincible against the Jedi. He became Supreme Commander of the droid armies.

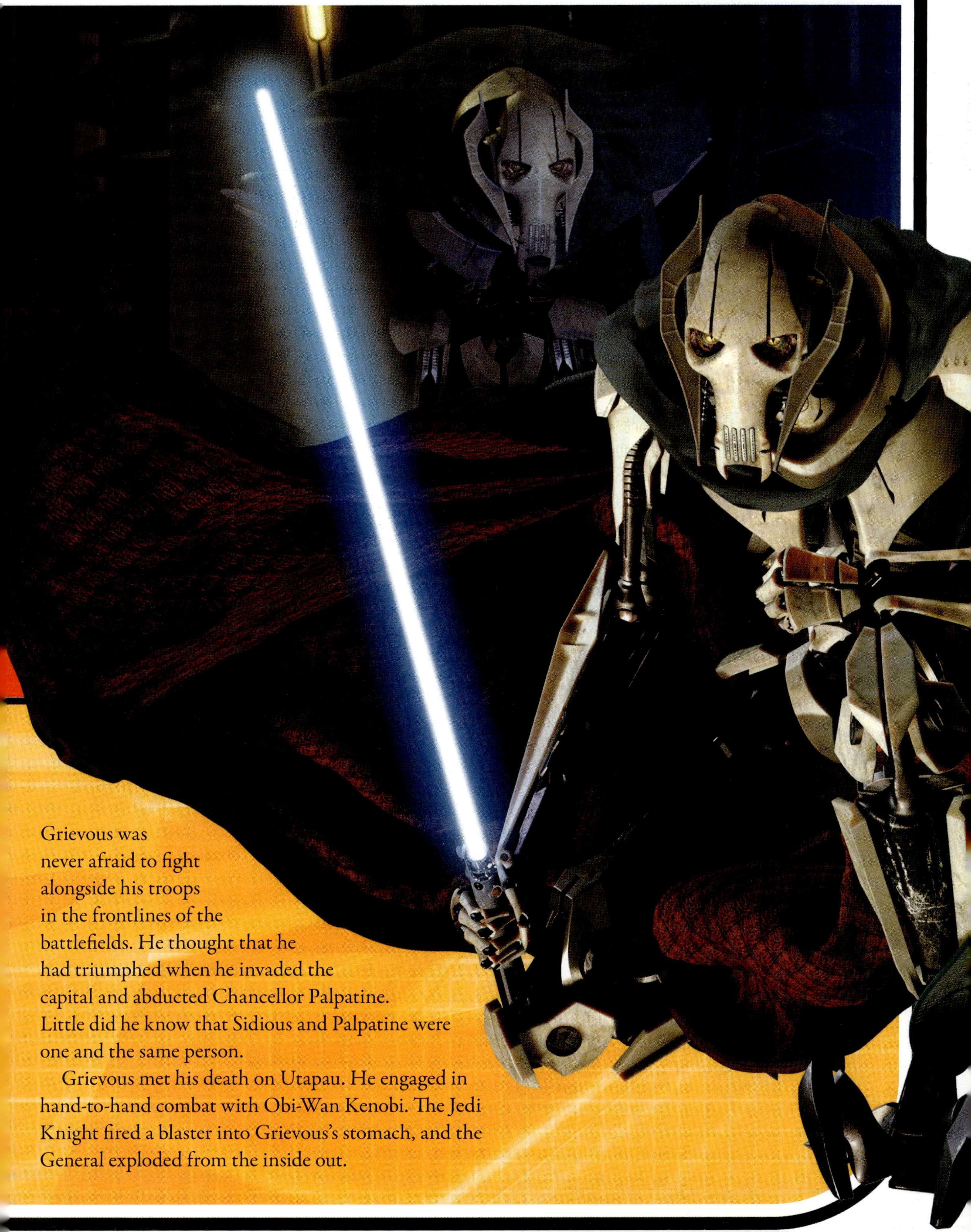

Grievous was never afraid to fight alongside his troops in the frontlines of the battlefields. He thought that he had triumphed when he invaded the capital and abducted Chancellor Palpatine. Little did he know that Sidious and Palpatine were one and the same person.

Grievous met his death on Utapau. He engaged in hand-to-hand combat with Obi-Wan Kenobi. The Jedi Knight fired a blaster into Grievous's stomach, and the General exploded from the inside out.

STAR WARS

STAR WARS

Log book
STAR WARS

KEEP A LOG OF YOUR OWN ADVENTURES THIS SUMMER. USE THIS SPACE TO RECORD THE EVENTS OF EACH DAY.

Most exciting moment of the summer:

....

....

....

LOG IN

NAME

....

....

....

....

....

....

....

....

....

....

....

....

....

....

....

....

....

....

....

....

....

....

....

....

....

....

....

....

....

....

....

....

....

LOG OUT

Top five locations of the summer:

1. ....

....

2. ....

....

3. ....

....

4. ....

....

5. ....

....

My most vivid dream:

....

I think it means:

....

WHAT'S IN A WORD?

HOW MANY NEW WORDS CAN YOU MAKE FROM THE NAME DARTH VADER?

1. ....
2. ....
3. ....
4. ....
5. ....
6. ....
7. ....
8. ....
9. ....
10. ....
11. ....
12. ....
13. ....
14. ....
15. ....
16. ....
17. ....
18. ....
19. ....
20. ....
21. ....
22. ....
23. ....
24. ....
25. ....
26. ....
27. ....
28. ....
29. ....
30. ....

SCRAMBLE

CAN YOU UNSCRAMBLE THESE LETTERS AND FIND THE HIDDEN PHRASES AND NAMES?

1. EFEL HET CERFO.

....

2. RALENEG VORGIEUS.

....

3. HIMS WERSLKAKY.

....

4. A LAXYGA RFA, ARF YAAW.

....

5. ETH NUMMLEINLI LCFONA.

....

6. STEAMR ACME DIUNW.

....

7. INPALATEP SI RTDHA OUDISIS.

....

8. HET RDKA IDES.

....

9. ETH NECSHO OEN.

....

10. TEH ONCLE SARW.

....

LANDO CALRISSIAN

HOMEWORLD:	UNKNOWN
SPECIES:	HUMAN
WEAPON:	HOLD-OUT BLASTER
VEHICLE:	MILLENNIUM FALCON; LADY LUCK,
AFFILIATION:	REBEL ALLIANCE

Lando Calrissian was a suave gambler, an ex-pirate and a sophisticated businessman. He had known Han Solo for many years, and the *Millennium Falcon* had passed between them over several games of sabacc. Han won the ship in the end (although Lando maintained that he cheated).

When Lando became the baron administrator of Bespin's Cloud City, he turned his back on smuggling and chose to be a legitimate businessman. However, when Darth Vader turned up, Lando was forced to betray Han Solo.

Although Lando thought that he was protecting his people, he soon realised that he had been set up. He freed Leia and Chewbacca and alerted the citizens of Cloud City to the threat of the Empire. Then he set off to rescue Han Solo, once again on the wrong side of the law.

Eventually, Lando sneaked into the palace of Jabba the Hutt disguised as a skiff guard. Jabba had Han Solo prisoner, and Lando was waiting for Luke Skywalker, who was now highly skilled, and almost a Jedi Knight. Although at first it seemed that their plan had failed, the repulsive gangster had bitten off far more than he could chew. Lando played a vital role in the destruction of the infamous Jabba the Hutt.

Lando's part in the rescue of Han Solo and his piloting abilities gained him the commission of General within the ranks of the Rebel Alliance. Lando led the attack on the second Death Star, commanding the Rebel starfighters as Gold Leader.

When Han Solo's team had destroyed the shield generator protecting the Death Star, Lando fired several missiles into the battle station's core reactor, destroying it. Lando was a hero and the Empire was crushed at last.

Light Side

Word Search

Seek out all ten light-side words in this word search. Answers can be forwards, backwards, vertical, horizontal or diagonal.

A	L	D	E	F	B	K	A	M	F	L	F	I	J	D
H	C	O	G	E	G	A	R	U	O	C	B	C	F	P
S	B	H	H	L	C	A	M	D	B	H	J	A	E	E
K	D	K	T	P	A	T	I	E	N	C	E	F	M	E
Y	N	E	G	G	B	H	B	Q	H	N	L	D	Y	K
W	A	H	N	E	Q	A	K	K	O	E	B	D	N	I
A	G	N	E	K	C	Q	G	I	D	F	Q	L	I	G
L	C	E	R	I	D	P	S	G	B	A	N	H	T	M
K	P	B	T	C	K	S	F	D	E	Q	B	Q	S	J
E	D	Q	S	Q	A	G	L	B	S	L	F	E	E	G
R	I	B	E	P	D	O	F	F	C	U	A	N	D	O
P	L	I	M	Q	E	B	A	L	G	J	C	D	B	I
C	F	O	H	F	D	M	I	A	D	J	Y	O	D	A
D	C	L	V	A	D	M	T	B	E	C	G	N	F	O
B	E	C	F	E	E	H	H	J	M	A	D	J	F	G

- ☐ COMPASSION
- ☐ COURAGE
- ☐ DESTINY
- ☐ FAITH
- ☐ FOCUS
- ☐ LOVE
- ☐ PATIENCE
- ☐ SKYWALKER
- ☐ STRENGTH
- ☐ YODA

KAKURO

Are you clever enough to solve this Kakuro puzzle?

- There are numbers in the orange squares. These numbers are called clues.
- Some squares are divided by a diagonal slash. The number in the top right corner is an 'across' clue. The number in the bottom left corner is a 'down' clue.
- You must insert numbers from 1 to 9 into the white squares to add up to the clue.
- You can't repeat any number twice in the same entry.

■	■	↓9	■	■	↓16	■
→8			→3 ↓19			■
■	→17			↓14		■
■	■	→24 ↓6				■
■	→6				↓4	■
■	■		→5			■
■	→4			→3		

HINT :: Start off with the '4' clues!

CHARACTER STRENGTH

COULD THE DARK SIDE SEDUCE YOU?

ANSWER THESE QUESTIONS TO FIND OUT.

QUESTION 01

HAVE YOU EVER CHEATED IN A TEST OR EXAM?

- **A** :: Yes ☐
- **B** :: No ☐
- **C** :: Once but never again ☐

QUESTION 02

HAVE YOU EVER CHEATED IN A GAME?

- **A** :: Yes ☐
- **B** :: No ☐
- **C** :: Once but never again ☐

QUESTION 03

DO YOU AGREE THAT THE MEANS JUSTIFY THE END?

- **A ::** Yes ☐
- **B ::** No ☐
- **C ::** Sometimes ☐

QUESTION 04

WHO WOULD YOU TRUST MORE, SOMEONE DRESSED IN A SMART SUIT OR SOMEONE DRESSED IN DIRTY, TORN CLOTHES?

- **A ::** Smart suit ☐
- **B ::** Torn clothes ☐
- **C ::** It would depend on what my instincts told me ☐

QUESTION 05

WOULD YOU GET A THRILL FROM THE DANGER OF A SWIFT LIGHTSABER DUEL?

- **A ::** No ☐
- **B ::** Yes ☐
- **C ::** I don't know ☐

QUESTION 06

WOULD YOU DO ANYTHING TO PROTECT YOUR FAMILY?

- **A ::** Yes ☐
- **B ::** No, not 'anything' ☐
- **C ::** I would have to see how I felt at the time ☐

QUESTION 07

ARE YOU AMBITIOUS?

- **A ::** Yes, very ☐
- **B ::** Not at all ☐
- **C ::** I am ambitious for happiness and peace ☐

QUESTION 08

WHEN WAS THE LAST TIME YOU LOST YOUR TEMPER?

- **A ::** I can't remember ☐
- **B ::** Less than a week ago ☐
- **C ::** More than a week ago ☐

QUESTION 09

DO YOU HAVE A LOT OF FEARS?

- **A ::** Yes ☐
- **B ::** No ☐
- **C ::** Only one or two major fears ☐

QUESTION 10

HOW IMPORTANT IS SELF CONTROL?

- **A ::** Extremely ☐
- **B ::** Fairly ☐
- **C ::** Not very ☐

USE THIS TABLE TO WORK OUT YOUR SCORE.

	A	B	C
1	10	0	5
2	10	0	5
3	10	0	5
4	10	5	0
5	0	10	5
6	10	0	5
7	10	5	0
8	0	10	5
9	10	0	5
10	0	5	10

0-10

YOU WILL MAKE A SUPERB JEDI KNIGHT. YOU ARE CALM, THOUGHTFUL AND ALWAYS THINK THINGS THROUGH. THE SITH HAVE NO CHANCE OF CORRUPTING YOU!

15-50

YOU WILL NEED TO PUT UP A FIGHT TO RESIST THE LURE OF THE DARK SIDE. HOWEVER, THE STRONGER PART OF YOUR NATURE WILL HELP YOU, AND YOU WILL SUCCEED IN TURNING AWAY FROM THE SITH.

55-100

BEWARE! YOU ARE STRAYING DOWN A DANGEROUS PATH. BE CAREFUL OF YOUR THOUGHTS AND FEELINGS, OR YOU WILL FIND THAT YOU CANNOT PULL AWAY FROM THE DARK SIDE.

PRINCESS LEIA ORGANA

HOMEWORLD:	ALDERAAN
SPECIES:	HUMAN
WEAPON:	SPORTING BLASTER PISTOL
VEHICLE:	*TANTIVE IV*
AFFILIATION:	REBEL ALLIANCE, NEW REPUBLIC, GALACTIC ALLIANCE

Leia was the daughter of Padmé Amidala and Anakin Skywalker. She was born at the moment when Darth Sidious's plans to defeat the Jedi and destroy the Republic finally came about. It was vital that her existence, and that of her twin brother, Luke, should be hidden from Darth Vader and Emperor Palpatine.

Leia was brought up by Bail Organa, the Viceroy and First Chairman of the planet Alderaan. She was raised as his child and followed in the footsteps of her adoptive father when she entered into politics. Leia became the youngest member of the Imperial Senate.

Leia used her diplomatic immunity to carry supplies and information for the Rebels. She was a bold and decisive leader, with all her mother's diplomatic skill and razor-sharp intelligence. However, when she set out to take the blueprints of the Imperial Death Star to Obi-Wan

Kenobi, she fell foul of Darth Vader. Leia was interrogated, but she resisted Darth Vader's mind probes. Little did either of them guess that it was because he was her father, and had passed on to her his strength and resilience.

Leia fell in love with the space pirate, Han Solo, even though at first she found him rude and arrogant, and he thought her ungrateful and stuck up. When Jabba the Hutt held Han prisoner, Leia risked her life to save him. However, there was no time to indulge their feelings, because the Empire was building a second Death Star. Only when the evil Emperor and his corrupt Empire were destroyed could Leia and Han finally declare their true feelings for each other.

WEAPONRY DESIGN STATION:

Stormtrooper armour

Use this grid to make your own technical drawing of the formidable

Stormtrooper armour.

JEDI CROSSWORD

WITH YOUR JEDI SKILLS, THESE CLUES SHOULD BE EASY TO SOLVE.

DOWN

1. A JEDI'S WEAPON.
3. WHO KILLED BOBA'S FATHER?
5. A JEDI MASTER'S APPRENTICE.
6. CHEWBACCA'S HOME PLANET.

ACROSS

2. __________ SKYWALKER CREATED C-3PO.
4. THE RACE THAT KILLED SHMI.
7. THE PLANET WHERE LEIA GREW UP.
8. LUKE'S MOTHER WAS PADMÉ __________.

CODE WRITING

SOMETIMES IT IS VITAL TO BE ABLE TO COMMUNICATE SECRETLY WITH YOUR COLLEAGUES. HERE IS A SIMPLE BUT EFFECTIVE CODE THAT WILL ALLOW YOU TO SEND MESSAGES SECURELY, BECAUSE THEY WILL ONLY MAKE SENSE TO SOMEONE ELSE WHO HOLDS THE CODEBREAKER.

MAYBE AND YELL STOOD HERE BEND
FIVE FOLDER RED UNCLE SLEEVE
BE GREEN UNWIND PICK ESTUARY HAT
YOUR PONY SUNNY

1. Lay a ruler across a sheet of paper.
2. Write your message, but space out the letters. There should be one letter at every half-inch mark.
3. Put a dot underneath the last letter of your message.
4. Fill in random letters in the spaces to make new words that don't relate to your message.

To read the message, your colleague should put a ruler under the letters with the final letter over a half-inch mark. Now he or she can read the letters that appear every half-inch.

YODA'S

JEDI TRIALS

You have reached the final stage of your training. Do not allow fear to take control now.

Your destiny is in your hands.

Question 13

A YOUNGER PADAWAN COMES TO YOU FOR ADVICE. WHAT DO YOU DO?

- A :: FEEL PLEASED THAT HE HAS CHOSEN YOU AND YOU TRY TO ADVISE HIM WISELY ☐
- B :: REFUSE TO LISTEN TO HIS TROUBLES – HE SHOULD BE SPEAKING TO HIS MASTER ☐
- C :: LISTEN CAREFULLY AND TRY TO PERSUADE HIM TO TALK TO HIS MASTER ☐

Question 14

YOU LOSE YOUR TEMPER COMPLETELY DURING YOUR TRAINING. HOW DO YOU TRY TO REGAIN SELF CONTROL?

- A :: MEDITATION ☐
- B :: LET THE ANGER OUT BY YELLING AND RELEASING PENT-UP TENSION ☐
- C :: BITE YOUR LIP AND COUNT TO TEN ☐

Question 15

YOUR MASTER IS ACTING STRANGELY. WHAT DO YOU DO?

- A :: ASK HIM IF SOMETHING IS WRONG ☐
- B :: REPORT HIM TO THE COUNCIL AT ONCE ☐
- C :: WAIT AND SEE, BUT KEEP A CLOSE EYE ON HIM ☐

Question 16

WHAT DOES LOVE MEAN TO YOU?

- A :: MARRIAGE ☐
- B :: DEVOTION TO A PARTNER ☐
- C :: OVERWHELMING EMOTION ☐

Question 17

OUT OF FRIENDS, FAMILY AND THE FORCE, WHICH COMES FIRST?

- A :: FRIENDS ☐
- B :: FAMILY ☐
- C :: FORCE ☐

Question 18

YOUR BEST FRIEND HAS TURNED TO THE DARK SIDE AND HAS TO BE STOPPED, EVEN IF THAT MEANS KILLING HER. HOW DO YOU FEEL ABOUT TAKING THE MISSION?

- A :: YOU REFUSE TO DO IT ☐
- B :: YOU ARE ANGRY AND YOU WANT REVENGE ON HER ☐
- C :: YOU ARE DEEPLY SADDENED, BUT YOU HOPE TO FIND A WAY OF SAVING HER ☐

Now you have completed your training!

ADD UP ALL YOUR SCORES TO DISCOVER HOW SKILLED A JEDI YOU HAVE BECOME.

13.	A=2	B=6	C=10
14.	A=10	B=2	C=6
15.	A=6	B=2	C=10
16.	A=6	B=10	C=2
17.	A=6	B=2	C=10
18.	A=6	B=2	C=10

WRITE DOWN YOUR SCORE HERE!

....

FINAL RESULTS

170-180 :: YOU HAVE BEEN ASKED TO JOIN THE JEDI COUNCIL.

150-170 :: YOU HAVE DEVELOPED EXCEPTIONAL FORCE SKILLS AND ARE NOW A JEDI MASTER.

100-150 :: CONGRATULATIONS, YOU HAVE ACHIEVED THE RANK OF A JEDI KNIGHT.

PAGE 14

Bail Organa → Alderaan
Chewbacca → Kashyyyk
Count Dooku → Serenno
Jabba the Hutt → Tatooine
Jar Jar Binks → Naboo
Lama Su → Kamino
Nute Gunray → Neimoidia
Wicket W. Warrick → Endor's forest moon

PAGE 15

A	F	D	E	R	E	H	S	D	G	E	B	K	M	H
C	B	H	A	I	K	E	R	H	D	N	C	N	A	M
E	M	G	N	I	N	T	H	G	I	L	D	S	O	I
I	H	O	B	O	E	F	G	B	I	C	R	B	K	A
F	L	B	L	J	H	C	I	K	A	E	E	D	I	D
B	H	C	O	D	T	G	E	M	P	E	R	O	R	K
Q	E	R	B	F	I	G	I	O	K	B	F	C	E	A
K	M	D	J	H	S	Q	O	C	E	A	G	F	G	N
J	P	G	D	H	L	R	B	J	I	D	A	E	N	J
B	I	Q	H	E	T	M	D	F	L	O	M	G	A	F
E	R	G	Q	M	I	B	A	C	J	O	I	E	H	N
Q	E	H	R	A	E	F	E	G	F	K	F	R	A	L
O	L	O	Q	G	R	I	E	V	O	U	S	C	R	E
H	T	J	B	N	E	R	J	E	R	F	C	L	J	I
S	Q	K	G	J	A	F	L	I	B	N	O	A	K	C

PAGE 26

1. OBI-WAN KENOBI
2. SITH
3. CORUSCANT
4. TATOOINE
5. WATTO
6. FORCE
7. PODRACE
8. SHMI
9. JEDI
10. DARTH SIDIOUS
11. COUNCIL
12. YODA
13. PADAWAN
14. PALPATINE
15. VALORUM
16. GUNGANS
17. THRONE ROOM
18. TORPEDO
19. TRADE FEDERATION
20. GALACTIC REPUBLIC
21. JEDI KNIGHT

PAGE 28

PAGE 29

PAGE 32

PAGE 33

5	9	4	8	6	2	1	3	7
6	3	1	4	7	9	8	2	5
2	8	7	3	1	5	4	6	9
3	2	8	6	5	1	9	7	4
7	5	9	2	3	4	6	8	1
1	4	6	7	9	8	2	5	3
9	7	5	1	2	6	3	4	8
4	6	3	9	8	7	5	1	2
8	1	2	5	4	3	7	9	6

PAGE 40

1. YOUR NAME.
2. A BANTHA'S SHADOW.
3. A RIVER.
4. A CARPET.
5. A STAMP.
6. A SPONGE.
7. LIGHT.
8. FIRE.
9. A MUSHROOM.
10. BREATH.
11. A SPLINTER.
12. A COAT OF PAINT.
13. 'ARE YOU ASLEEP?'

PAGE 41

1. SITH – SITE – SIDE – HIDE
2. SHIP – CHIP – CHIN – THIN – THIS
3. FEAR – DEAR – DEAD – MEAD – MEAN
4. STAR – SCAR – SCAM – SEAM – BEAM
5. LOVE – DOVE – DONE – BONE – BOND
6. CLONE – CRONE – DRONE – DROVE – PROVE
7. SPACE – SPARE – SCARE – SCALE – STALE – STALL – SMALL – SMELL

PAGES 44 – 45

The correct order is:
9, 6, 1, 5, 3, 8, 2, 10, 4, 12, 11, 7

PAGE 53

1. FEEL THE FORCE.
2. GENERAL GRIEVOUS.
3. SHMI SKYWALKER.
4. A GALAXY FAR, FAR AWAY.
5. THE MILLENNIUM FALCON.
6. MASTER MACE WINDU.
7. PALPATINE IS DARTH SIDIOUS.
8. THE DARK SIDE.
9. THE CHOSEN ONE.
10. THE CLONE WARS.

PAGE 56

A	L	D	E	F	B	K	A	M	F	L	F	I	J	D
H	C	O	G	E	G	A	R	U	O	C	B	C	F	P
S	B	H	H	L	C	A	M	D	B	H	J	A	E	E
K	D	K	T	P	A	T	I	E	N	C	E	F	M	E
Y	N	E	G	G	B	H	B	Q	H	N	L	D	Y	K
W	A	H	N	E	Q	A	K	K	O	E	B	D	N	I
A	G	N	E	K	C	Q	G	I	D	F	Q	L	I	G
L	C	E	R	I	D	P	S	G	B	A	N	H	T	M
K	P	B	T	C	K	S	F	D	E	Q	B	Q	S	J
E	D	Q	S	Q	A	G	L	B	S	L	F	E	E	G
R	I	B	E	P	D	O	F	F	C	U	A	N	D	O
P	L	I	M	Q	E	B	A	L	G	J	C	D	B	I
C	F	O	H	F	D	M	I	A	D	J	Y	O	D	A
D	C	L	V	A	D	M	T	B	E	C	G	N	F	O
B	E	C	F	E	E	H	H	J	M	A	D	J	F	G

PAGE 57

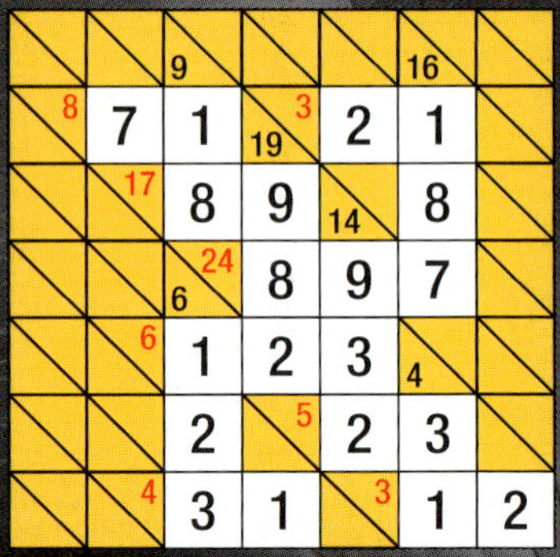

PAGE 64

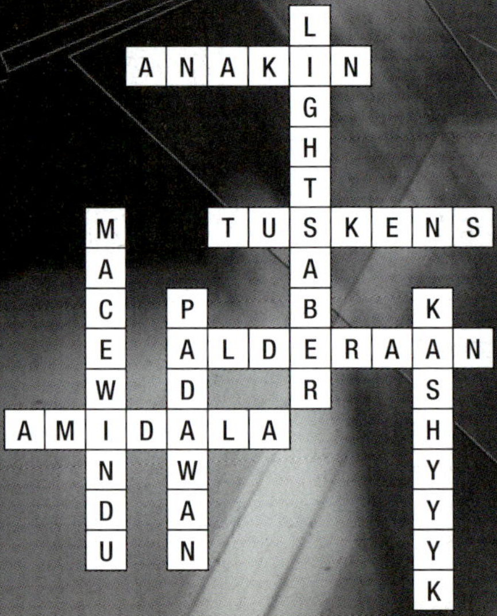